OLD-TIME

BASE BALL

and
the First
Modern
World
Series

Baseball used in the
first modern World Series game
October 1, 1903
Huntington Avenue Grounds, Boston

OLD-TIME
BASE BALL

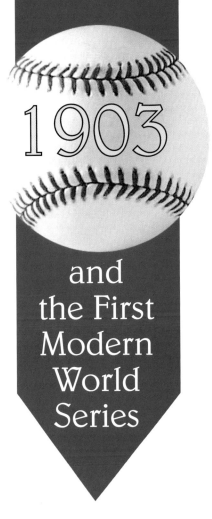

1903

and
the First
Modern
World
Series

The Millbrook Press
Brookfield, Connecticut

This book is dedicated my mom and dad.

Also to my friend Kathy Silvestri, who turned my rough manuscript into a presentable document.

But especially to my wife, Karen, and sons Seth, Jeremy, and Brendan.

Copyright © 2002 by Peter A. Campbell

Published by
The Millbrook Press, Inc.
2 Old New Milford Road
Brookfield, Connecticut 06804
www.millbrookpress.com

Printed in Hong Kong

5 4 3 2 1

Library of Congress Cataloging-in-Publication Data

Campbell, Peter A.
Old-time base ball and the first modern world series / written
and illustrated by Peter A. Campbell.
p. cm.
Includes index.
Summary: Chronicles baseball history from the first regulated game in 1846 to
the first World Series in 1903, including the development of the Major Leagues,
and profiles noteworthy players, owners, and parks.
ISBN 0-7613-2466-6 (lib. bdg.)
1. Baseball—United States—History—Juvenile literature. 2. World Series
(Baseball)—History—Juvenile literature. [1. Baseball—History. 2. World Series
(Baseball)—History.] I. Title: Oldtime baseball and the first modern World
Series. II. Title.

GV867.5.C36 2002
796.357′0973—dc21
2001045013

Picture Credits:

Boston Public Library—pp. 28, 36, 37 background photo of Huntington Avenue
Grounds; p. 38 Pittsburgh team in dugout; p. 39 fans climbing fence at
Huntington Avenue Grounds; pp. 42/43
background photo Exposition Park; p. 45 Pilgrims raise World Series flag 1904.
Baseball Hall of Fame Library, Cooperstown, NY—Cover,
background photo of Huntington Avenue Grounds pp. 1, 18, 27, 44; background
and inset photo of Huntington Avenue Grounds.
Carnegie Library of Pittsburgh—p. 35, 40, 41 background photo of Exposition
Park; p. 43 inset of smoke (retouched) over Exposition Park.
George Eastman House—p. 12 Lewis Hines Photo.
Binney & Smith (Crayola Crayons)—p. 16
Library of Congress—p. 38/39 background photo of Huntington Avenue
Grounds.
Collection of the Author—p. 2, 6, 26, 46.

Contents

1903

Chapter 1

Base Ball – The Early Years

A variation of traditional bat-and-ball games like "rounders," "base," and "old cat," baseball, can be traced back to colonial times. One of the earliest accounts of baseball in America is found in the journal of George Ewing, a soldier in General George Washington's army, encamped at Valley Forge, in 1778. On April 17 of that year, Ewing wrote that he and his fellow patriots had played a game of "Base." It was also reported that General Washington had played a similar game with his troops.

By the early 1800s, a popular version of "ball-and-stick" known as "townball" was being played in schoolyards, on village greens, and on college campuses across America. Each town played the game according to its own rules and formed its own teams, with some having as many as 18 players.

In 1823 the first reference to an organized game called "base ball"[*] appeared in a New York newspaper called the National Advocate.

In the 1840s, America was a thriving nation, due to its rapid expansion and accelerated population growth in cities along the East Coast. People living in these fast-growing cities began seeking new ways to spend their leisure time. With hunting and horse racing enjoyed by most of rural America, baseball seemed a practical alternative, since all it took to play the game was an open field, a bat, and a ball.

Quickly, baseball became not only a favorite sport but a "gentleman's game." Doctors, lawyers, shipbuilders, bankers, and undertakers were among the many who at midday would break free from their work routine to play a game of baseball. Less affluent members of society, however, had little time to indulge in such spirited leisure activity.

*The word "baseball" was originally spelled as two words up until the early 1900s.

Alexander Cartwright

In 1845, a 25-year-old New York bank teller and volunteer fireman devised a set of rules that helped define the game of baseball. His name was Alexander Cartwright.

Categorized by new guidelines, baseball soon distinguished itself from the earlier English games of rounders and cricket.

In September 1845, Cartwright formed the first baseball club in America — the New York Knickerbockers. Due to the absence of playing-field space in Manhattan, the Knickerbockers had to take a 15-minute ferry ride across the Hudson River to play baseball in Elysian Fields, a beautiful picnic grove located in Hoboken, New Jersey.

On June 19, 1846, baseball history was made at Elysian Fields when the New York Knickerbockers played the first baseball game according to Cartwright's rules. They lost to the New York Baseball Club, 23 to 1.

The popularity of Cartwright's regulated baseball, known as "the New York game," quickly spread throughout the East and became so admired that 300 copies of his baseball rulebook were printed for distribution. Cartwright was fast becoming baseball's "first teacher."

By the late 1850s, more than 100 teams were playing baseball in New Jersey. New York City alone was home to 50 baseball clubs. To broaden the game's appeal and encourage other states to participate in the sport, the first baseball league was formed in 1858. It was called the National Association of Base Ball Players.

In 1861, the nation was embroiled in the bitter Civil War. Organized baseball came to a standstill, while young men from the North and rural South trudged off to join a battle that would determine the fate of a nation. Between the bloody battles that took place at Bull Run, Antietam, Fredericksburg, and Gettysburg, soldiers from both sides of the Civil War found time to learn and play baseball. On campgrounds in the North and South baseball's appeal grew in popularity.

At the end of the Civil War in 1865, Northern and Southern soldiers returned to mill towns, big cities, farms, and small towns across America taking home with them — baseball.

By the late 1860s, baseball was quickly evolving into our national pastime.

In 1869, Henry Wright created the first paid professional baseball team, the Cincinnati Red Stockings. Each baseball player received a salary.

Elysian Fields

Henry's brother, George, the team's shortstop, received the highest salary — $1,400. That season, the Cincinnati Red Stockings won 65 games and lost none.

With the exception of the Cincinnati Red Stockings, Baseball was played purely as an amateur sport until 1871 when the National Association of Professional Base Ball Players was formed. By 1875, the league was in trouble and with it, baseball. Gambling and the sale of alcohol infiltrated ballparks, disgusting and angering many of its fans.* They began staying away from the ballparks in large numbers.

In 1876, businessman William Hulbert helped save baseball by purchasing the failing National Association of Professional Base Ball Players. Hulbert and other baseball team owners implemented new rules to bring respectability back to the game. There would be no more drinking, gambling, or baseball games on Sundays. Fans would be charged 50 cents admission to a ballpark to see a game. He renamed the organization the National League.

With the success of the National League came the birth of its counterpart, the American Association. The newly created "league" charged only 25 cents for fans to attend a ballpark and permitted alcohol and Sunday ball games.

As the leagues grew more substantial, baseball team owners wanted more control over their ballplayers and instituted a "reserve clause" in their contracts. This clause enabled an owner to automatically renew a ballplayer's salary agreement with him and prevented the ballplayer from engaging in salary negotiations with rival baseball teams. Baseball team owners literally owned the services of ballplayers, and kept them from being exchanged or traded unless they permitted it.

This new baseball salary arrangement angered ballplayers in both leagues, and many sought retaliation by forming new leagues between 1884 and 1890, all of which failed miserably. To make matters worse,

*Male fans were called "cranks" or "bugs," and women, "crankettes."

the American Association failed, due to the loss of many of its best ballplayers and revenue that went to rival leagues.

Only one baseball league—the National League—composed of 12 teams and owned by Albert Goodwill Spalding, remained. Once again, baseball was in serious trouble. Greedy baseball team owners, disenchanted ballplayers, and dispirited fans stopped visiting ballparks. Low attendance resulted in lost revenue.

Despite all the problems surrounding baseball at the turn of the century, baseball was about to undergo a remarkable transformation into the modern game we know today.

By the late 1880s baseball was being played all across America. Uniforms of all styles and colors were in vogue.

Chapter 2

A New Century– The Birth of Modern-Day Baseball

It's the dawn of the 20th century in America. The United States, now composed of 45 states, has a population of 76 million citizens. Dirt roads and horse-drawn carriages still grace the nation's landscape, and an 1890 census declares the American frontier closed.

It has been 10 years since the massacre of the Lakota Sioux Indians by the U.S. Cavalry at Wounded Knee, South Dakota, on December 29, 1890, an event that brought an end to bloody Indian wars fought across America.

It is a time of great change.

On September 1, 1901, the newly elected president of the United States, William McKinley, was shot and killed by an assassin. His vice president, Theodore "Teddy" Roosevelt, took the oath of office to become the nation's 26th president. At 42 years of age, the youngest president in United States history, Roosevelt proved to be a man of action. He advocated old-age pensions, child-labor laws, a national conservation system, and women's suffrage and transformed a conservative nation into one primed for progress.

In the early years of the century, great contributions were being made in the fields of science,[*] art, and literature.

At Kitty Hawk, North Carolina, two brothers, Wilbur and Orville Wright, took humanity skyward with their first airplane flight. In his film studio the inventor Thomas Edison produced the first silent motion

---

[*]*The great Age of Invention (1870–1920). During this period the lightbulb, automobile, airplane, movies, and the telephone were invented.*

picture: *The Great Train Robbery.* It ran for 20 minutes. The chemists Madame Marie Curie and her husband, Pierre, were awarded

the Nobel Prize for
their joint research on radiation; and
Booker T. Washington, the American educator and
author of the poignant autobiography *Up from Slavery,* became the
first black American to dine at the White House.

America's progress at the turn of the century did not go
unnoticed, as a new wave of immigrants emigrated from Russia,
Italy, Poland, and Greece and began to settle in small mill towns and
crowded cities around the country.

But this shining nation of bright promise held no streets
lined with gold, contrary to what many believed. Life in
America was not easy. The country's newest immigrants
found low wages, poor working conditions, and an

Booker T. Washington

average workweek of 60 hours as their American dream turned into a harsh reality.

Breaking through the doom and gloom of the miserable living and working conditions that greeted these immigrants to America were "lighter" diversions. The circus, vaudeville, Wild West shows, and expositions helped take the immigrants' minds off the day-to-day drudgery of making a living. But it was baseball that seemed to capture the very heart and rugged spirit of their new American homeland. Played by professional ballplayers on a fields of green grass, this exhilarating sport seemed to catapult their spirits to a higher plane, providing them with a sweet escape from the grim shops and dreary factories that governed their daily lives.

By 1900, having survived challenges from organizations like the Union Association, the American Association, and the Players League, the National League controlled professional baseball.

The League had whittled itself down from 12 teams to 8 and held a formidable grip on its ballplayers.

Baseball team owners showed ballplayers little respect.

No ballplayer earned more than $2,500 for a season of play, and the "reserve clause" in each ballplayer's contract flatly stated that he must play his entire professional career with one team.

Baseball fans fared no better. Gambling and drinking returned to ballparks, and cheating and rough play were tolerated — even umpires endured verbal abuse and physical assaults. Fans began staying away. And, with only 8 professional teams competing for the championship, fan interest fell off by the summer months of June and July. Baseball was losing its magic. To hundreds of fans, it seemed that professional baseball was on the very verge of collapse. A savior was needed.

In 1884, a 28-year-old sports editor from the *Cincinnati Commercial*

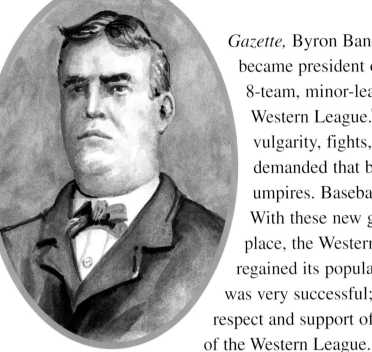

Gazette, Byron Bancroft "Ban" Johnson, became president of a struggling, rowdy, 8-team, minor-league circuit called the Western League.* Johnson outlawed vulgarity, fights, and rough play and demanded that ballplayers respect umpires. Baseball fans took notice. With these new guidelines in place, the Western League regained its popularity. Johnson was very successful; he gained the respect and support of almost all the owners of the Western League.

Bancroft "Ban" Johnson

By 1899, Johnson believed that his revitalized minor-league teams of the Western League could compete on a professional level with the troubled National League. He now knew it was time to make a move. He renamed the Western League the American League. At first, the National League dismissed the young opportunist, but Bancroft "Ban" Johnson was not to be ignored. He quickly moved some of his American League teams to cities like Baltimore, Washington, and Philadelphia and at times competed directly with the National League.

People were clearly watching, but it was Johnson's American League rejection of the reserve clause that finally raised eyebrows and caught serious attention from National League baseball team owners and disgruntled ballplayers.

By the end of the 1900 baseball season, many National League ballplayers considered switching to the American League. By the time the American League began its 1901 season, more than 100 National League ballplayers had defected to the American League. Cy Young,

Binney & Smith C help make the wor a more colorful place when they introduce Crayol Crayons in 1903.

The minor-league teams of the Western League were the Chicago White Stockings, Milwaukee Brewers, Indianapolis Hoosiers, Detroit Tigers, Kansas City Blues, Cleveland Lake Shores, Buffalo Bisons, and Minneapolis Millers.

Jimmy Collins, Larry Lajoie, and Joe McGinnity were among the many who joined the new league.

Johnson continued to penetrate National League territory. On January 28, 1901, Johnson abandoned his Buffalo franchise and placed a team in Boston, Massachusetts—a team that would later be known as the Boston Red Sox.

The rivalry between the two leagues continued until 1903, when an agreement was reached by the National League to formally acknowledge the American League. Bancroft "Ban" Johnson had succeeded in breaking the grip that greedy National League baseball team owners had held on baseball. Fans began returning to ballparks to support the new American League, and once again, baseball was the most exciting game in town.

At the beginning of the 20th century black Americans were barred from playing professional baseball. But this did not discourage them from playing. In 1920 the Negro National League was created.

Chapter 3

The Dead-Ball Era

With the creation of the American League in 1901 and its status as a professional franchise in 1903, the modern game of baseball had arrived.

In 1903, each league was composed of 8 teams. National League teams were located in Boston, Brooklyn, Chicago, Cincinnati, New York, Philadelphia, Pittsburgh, and St. Louis. The American League boasted teams in Boston, Chicago, Cleveland, Detroit, New York, Philadelphia, St. Louis and Washington.

By the close of the 19th century, baseball had undergone some dramatic changes. In 1884, for the first time, the pitcher was allowed to throw a baseball overhand. (Prior to this time, ballplayers had to pitch a baseball using an underhand toss.) In 1888, the "three-strikes-and-you're-out" rule was established. In 1893, one of the most dramatic rule changes occurred when the pitching mound was repositioned from 55 feet (1,676 centimeters) to 60 feet 6 inches (1,844 centimeters) away from home plate. The purpose was to give ballplayers better hitting odds against fastball pitchers of the day, like Christy Mathewson and Cy Young. That same year, batting averages rose more than 30 percent. In 1900, the shape of home plate changed from a 12-inch (30-centimeter) square to the five-sided pentagon shape we know today. By 1901, the modern game of baseball was in full swing.

In the late 1800s and early 1900s, old-time baseball was referred to as the "Dead-Ball Era."[*] Baseballs used during this period were made of horsehide with a vulcanized rubber center tightly wound with yarn. Only one baseball was used during a game. If the baseball was hit or thrown into the stands during a baseball game, fans were asked to throw the baseball back onto the ball field. As you might imagine, very few home runs were hit by ballplayers during the Dead-Ball Era. Power hitters of the day would average 10 to 20 home runs in a season.

---

[*]*The "Dead-Ball Era" began in the late 1800s and ended in 1920, when Babe Ruth, of the New York Yankees, hit 54 home runs. The growth in the number of home runs in 1920 was due in no small part to the introduction of a "livelier" baseball and the use of more than one baseball during a ball game.*

The type of game played during the Dead-Ball Era was different, too. Since a baseball could not often be hit for a long distance, it became vital for baseball teams to devise strategies and tactics that would help them score points during a ball game. Bunting, hit-and-run plays, and base stealing made up a team's offensive strategy. These three methods of scoring runs evolved in the 1890s.

Ballplayers like Wee Willie Keeler of Baltimore (National League) took the art of bunting to whole new level. Despite weighing only 140 pounds (63 kilograms) and standing 5 feet 4 inches (162 centimeters) tall, Keeler was a force to be reckoned with at the plate. As a pitcher hurled a pitch to him, Keeler, feigning to bunt, would slide his hands halfway up his bat, then carefully pop a hit over the charging infielder's head. If infielders played him back or "deep," he would employ an innovative technique that allowed him to chop down on the baseball, bouncing it high off the firm Baltimore infield. Hits like these became

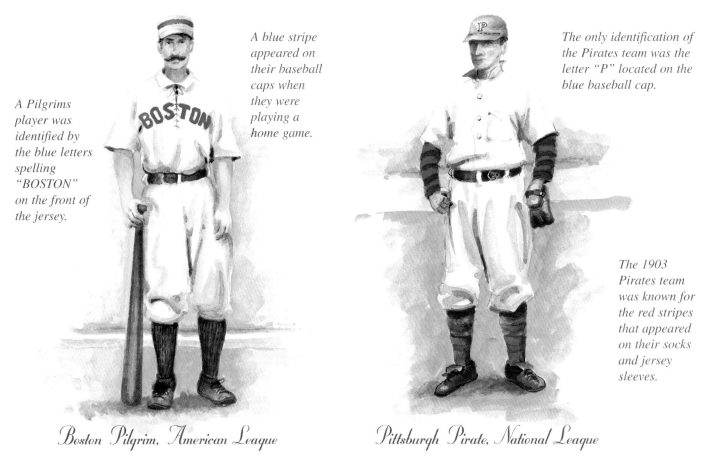

A Pilgrims player was identified by the blue letters spelling "BOSTON" on the front of the jersey.

A blue stripe appeared on their baseball caps when they were playing a home game.

The only identification of the Pirates team was the letter "P" located on the blue baseball cap.

The 1903 Pirates team was known for the red stripes that appeared on their socks and jersey sleeves.

Boston Pilgrim, American League   Pittsburgh Pirate, National League

The players' uniforms were made of 8 ounces (227 grams) of wool (washed only once a week). They usually wore them a size larger than the ballplayer's actual size, making it easier for ballplayers to pitch, field, hit, and run.

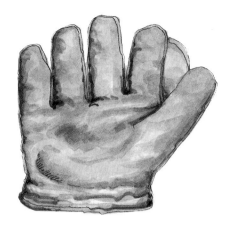

By the late 1800s the first fingerless glove is being worn.

By 1900 the glove offers more protection for the hand and fingers.

By 1903 a small web is added to help improve the players' fielding.

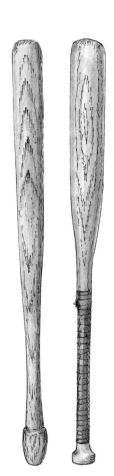

Early-style baseball bats.

(left) Late 1800 model called the "mushroom bat." (right) The "bottle bat" was popular in the early 1900s.

known as "Baltimore chops," and combined with Keeler's tremendous speed, helped him pump out many infield hits.

Another way of putting runs on the scoreboard was the hit-and-run play. How it works is the player on first base, with 1 or 2 outs, breaks for second base while the batter attempts to hit the ball into a gap created by the second baseman, who is forced to cover second because of the attempted stolen base. The Chicago White Stockings of the 1890s, led by Cap Anson and King Kelly, pioneered the art of the hit-and-run.

Base stealing became another important offensive maneuver. Ballplayers like William "Dummy" Hoy of Cincinnati, so named because he could neither hear nor speak, and the great Honus Wagner of Pittsburgh each tallied more than 600 stolen bases throughout their baseball careers.

In 1903, the American and National Leagues ruled that "home" baseball teams (baseball teams that played in their own cities) had to wear white uniforms, and visiting baseball teams (teams that visited from other cities to play against a home team) had to wear gray or black uniforms. The team's name might appear on the front of a baseball player's shirt.

Until the late 1800s, baseball players did not wear baseball gloves, because it was thought "unmanly." Ballplayers like Albert Goodwell Spalding, George Wright, and Al Reach changed that philosophy in 1877, when they donned "fingerless" baseball gloves made of buckskin to protect their hands while playing baseball. By the 1890s, the baseball glove had become standard equipment for every ballplayer.

Five-fingered baseball gloves used during the 1900s were crude-looking, small in size, and used solely to protect a ballplayer's fingers and hands from injury.

Pitchers of the Dead-Ball Era were a tough breed and were expected to pitch a ball game every two or three days. Baseball coaches demanded that pitchers finish an entire game, vehemently discouraging relief pitching. Pitchers, in turn, would resort to new methods to strike out a batter, including "doctoring," or altering, a baseball. A hidden piece of sandpaper to mar a baseball's surface created what was known as an "Emery ball." Talcum and paraffin were used to create a slick spot on a ball, known as a "Shine ball." Even chewing tobacco and licorice were used by infielders, who would chew either tobacco or licorice then spit into their baseball gloves, darkening the baseball's color and making it more difficult for a batter to spot a fast-pitched ball.

In the early 1900s only one umpire was used to officiate a game. In the 1903 World Series two were used in each game.

Umpires often used a common house broom to clean off the plate back then.

In 1882, the umpire became a very important part of the game of baseball. The American Association decided to pay umpires a salary and outfit them in uniforms that included a blue coat and cap. The National League instituted the same policy a year later. Only one umpire was allowed to participate in a ball game. His job was to announce or call "balls" and "strikes" from his position behind home plate. If a batter got on base, the umpire would often move to the pitcher's mound. From this location in the middle of the infield, he would have a better view of all the bases and home plate.

Ballplayers took advantage of this one-umpire system, and it was not uncommon for infielders to bump or trip base runners if they noticed that an umpire's attention was directed elsewhere on the playing field. A master at this "dirty" style of playing was John McGraw, third baseman for the Baltimore Orioles, who played during the 1890s. It wasn't until 1909 that both the American and National Leagues would officially require that more than one umpire oversee baseball games.

In 1901, baseball was clearly back in swing, thanks to "Ban" Johnson, then the most powerful man in the sport. There was no profanity, no fighting, no rough play, no verbal or physical abuse of umpires, and no alcohol permitted in ballparks.

By 1903, both the National and American Leagues agreed to play by the same rules and established baseball guidelines called "Joint Playing Rules."

With two well-established leagues, governed by a new, stricter set of rules, baseball was ready to soar to new heights.

THE TROUBLE AT BOSTON MUCH TO BE DEPLORED

Foreign Ownership Policy of the American League Caused Friction—Pittsburg Boys Should Win the Coming Series.

BATTLE OF THE GIANTS.

Providence vs. Metropolitans for the Championship of America.

Radbourn's Curves Enigmas to the New Yorkers.

The American Association Leaders Completely Shut Out.

Providence, 6; Metropolitan, 0.

NEW YORK, Oct. 23.—The Providence League champions and the Metropolitans, of this city, the champions of the American Association, played the first of a series of games for the championship of the United States, at the Polo grounds to-day. Great interest was felt in the contest, and over 2500 persons assembled to witness the game. The disagreeable weather was the means of keeping away probably three times the number present. A cold, raw wind blew across the grounds with considerable force, and made even the players shiver at times, and prevented any fine play. This was particularly the case with the home nine, who played far below the usual standard. Keefe pitched a miserable game, occasion-

REORGANIZATION OF AMERICAN BALL LEAGUE

Expansion Into a Major League is Completed at the Chicago Meeting.

SEASON WILL BE SAME AS LAST YEAR

New Plan Does Away With "Farming" of Players.

"Bunt" Hit May Be Abolished— President Johnson Says the League Will Go Ahead Regardless of Other Organizations.

"CY" YOUNG HAD THE PIRATE BATSMEN AT HIS MERCY

Chapter 4

The First "Modern" World Series

The first official world series between two baseball leagues was played in 1884 between the Providence Grays and the New York Metropolitans. The Providence Grays of the National League had finished the season in first place by 10½ games. Much of their success had to do with their ace pitcher Charles "Old Hoss" Radbourn who had totaled an incredible 60 wins for the season.

The new rival league, the American Association, also had a pennant winner in the New York Metropolitans. Jim Mutrie, manager of the New York team, felt that his team could beat the best of the National League. He offered a challenge to Frank Bancroft, manager of the Providence Grays, suggesting that the two teams play a 3-game "world series" at the Met's ballpark. Bankcroft and his Grays accepted the challenge.

Although the two teams only played 3 games, the postseason meeting between the National League and the American Association would be called the first "world series." The Providence Grays won all 3 games. "Old Hoss" Radbourn pitched all 3 games allowing only 3 runs.

The two leagues would continue to play a "world series" until the collapse of the American Association in 1890. The National League attempted to keep a postseason series "alive" by scheduling an Inter-League championship competition, but the concept

Charles "Old Hoss" Radbourn

failed to capture the interest of ballplayers and fans, and by 1898, "world series" play was no more.

The return of the "two-league" system in 1901 really saved baseball. "Ban" Johnson's creation of a new American League, coupled with his vision for a more respectable game, brought hundreds of fans back to the ballparks. One of the first attempts to revive postseason play came in 1902, when the National League Pittsburgh Pirates played a 4-game series against selected players from the new American League, called the All-Americans. Pittsburgh won 2 games; the All-Americans 1, and one game ended in a tie.

Although women were discouraged from playing baseball (considered too dangerous and not ladylike) in the early 1900s, this did not keep them from being enthusiastic fans of the game. These stylish fans were called crankettes.

In January 1903, one of the most important events in baseball occurred. A "National Agreement" was signed between the competing American and National Leagues. With this historic agreement, the National League recognized the American League as an equal. Both Leagues agreed to abide by the same rules of play. Finally, the Inter-League warfare for players and fans that had continued for more than two years had come to an end. With the agreement between the American and National Leagues, the modern game of baseball emerged.

By 1903, peace had returned to the Major Leagues, as they were now called. Ballpark attendance soared, and fans, or "cranks," responded enthusiastically to the competitive spirit created by the exciting two-league system. Throughout the season, the Boston Pilgrims[*] and the Pittsburgh Pirates dominated the game of baseball in their respective leagues — with Boston winning the American League pennant, 10 games ahead of Cleveland, to finish in first place. Pittsburgh, to no one's surprise, won its third-straight National League pennant.

At the end of the 1903 baseball season, cranks and sportswriters began to talk about a return to postseason play or a World Series. Barney Dreyfuss, owner of the Pittsburgh Pirates, quickly took up the

---

[*]*Since its formation in 1901, the Boston team has had numerous names: the Plymouth Rocks, the Somersets, and in 1903, the Pilgrims. Sportswriters and fans also knew the team as the Boston Americans. The Pittsburgh Pirates were also known as the Pittsburgh Nationals.*

call. Recognizing the potential for profitability that a World Series would create, Dreyfuss issued a World Series challenge to Henry Killilea, owner of the Boston Pilgrims. Equally quick to recognize the money to be made by such a competition, Killilea took up the offer and informed Dreyfuss that the Series was on. The two leagues agreed on a 9-game Series to commence on October 1.

The Series would end when one team had won 5 games. The first 3 games would be played in Boston, at Huntington Avenue Grounds. The next 4 games would be played in Pittsburgh at Exposition Park, and the last 2 games, if necessary, would be played back at Boston. Both team owners agreed to split any profits made from the Series equally.

Now the stage was set for the birth of the October classic that would forever be known as the first modern World Series.

A 1903 World Series souvenir card from game 2 played at the Huntington Avenue Grounds in Boston.

Chapter 5

The Two Teams and Their Ballparks

There was no doubt in the minds of sportswriters and baseball fans alike that, in 1903, the Boston Pilgrims and Pittsburgh Pirates were the best teams in baseball.

Boston Pilgrims

Formed in 1901, the Pilgrims team was part of the new American League and in its first year finished only 4 games behind first-place Chicago. The next year's season looked just as promising, until Jimmy Collins, the Pilgrims star third baseman and manager, injured his knee. Although Collins missed the second half of the season that year, the Pilgrims still managed to finish an impressive second place behind Philadelphia.

In 1903, everything came together for the Pilgrims. Armed with an outstanding pitching staff, strong defensive playing, and a formidable offense, the Pilgrims won their first American League pennant.

For three years, Charles Somers, the Pilgrims' owner, had assembled one of the best pitching staffs in baseball. Denton True Young, known to his teammates as "Cy" Young, the team's star pitcher, joined the Pilgrims in 1901 after spending two years with St. Louis. Given a three-year contract and a salary of $3,500, he was 34 years old when he joined Boston. Sportswriters and fans wondered whether Young was too old to become a winning pitcher for the Pilgrims. Their doubts were quickly dispelled.

Cy Young

In his first year, Cy helped the Pilgrims win 33 games, tallying more than 150 strikeouts. Fans rallied behind the pitching hero, and in no time he became a favorite player. In 1902, Young posted another 32 wins for the Boston team, for a total of 65 victories in two years.

The following year, 1903, Young threw 7 shutouts and added another 29 wins to his impressive game-win column. He was the best pitcher in baseball. But he wasn't the only star pitcher for the team from Boston.

In 1902, Charles Somers acquired Bill Dinneen from the Boston Beaneaters of the National League. Dinneen, who was also imposing on the pitcher's mound, won 21 games in 1902 and 1903.

Halfway through the 1902 season, right-handed pitcher Tom "Long Tom" Hughes, joined the Pilgrims and proved to be a valuable pitching starter, winning 20 games in 1903.

Cy Young's battery mate was catcher Lou Criger. Criger was a defensive specialist behind the plate and followed Young from Cleveland to St. Louis and ultimately to Boston in 1901.

Outstanding defensive play had also helped clinch the pennant for Boston that year. Jimmy Collins, Boston's star third baseman and manager, joined the Pilgrims in 1901 at a salary of $5,500. He was considered the best third baseman in baseball. Collins was joined by two talented minor leaguers, second baseman Albert "Hobe" Ferris and Freddy Parent, a tiny but gifted shortstop, who hit over .300 that season. Rounding out the defense was first baseman George "Candy" Lachance, who had been acquired from Cleveland to complete the Boston infield.

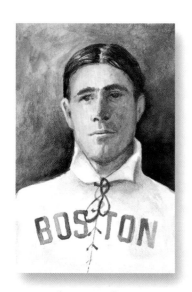

Jimmy Collins

Boston's offense was also a force to reckon with. Center fielder Charles "Chick" Stahl had a batting average of over .320 in his first two years with the team. John "Buck" Freeman, right fielder, led both Leagues with 13 home runs, finishing at the top in the American league for runs batted in in 1903. He was considered one of the great power hitters of his day.

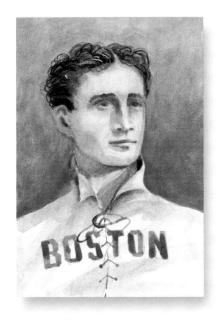

Patsy Dougherty

Patrolling left field was the great rookie prospect Patsy Dougherty, known for his speed in the outfield and on the base path. He was also no slouch at the plate, finishing the year with a .331 batting average.

The Pittsburgh Pirates

The strongest team in all baseball by the end of 1903 was none other than the Pittsburgh Pirates, who were coming off their third-straight National League pennant win. The year before, the Pirates had finished an amazing 27 ½ games ahead of Brooklyn, an accomplishment that actually hurt fan attendance in the National League.

When the Pirates team was formed in 1887, it was known as the Pittsburgh Alleghenies. After stealing second baseman Louis Bierbauer from the Philadelphia Athletics in 1889, the team renamed itself the Pirates. Barney Dreyfuss bought the team in 1900, along with 14 players from his defunct Louisville team. Included in the group were two future Hall of Famers, Honus Wagner and Fred Clarke. It was the beginning of one of the first great dynasties in baseball.

"Deacon" Phillippe

If Pittsburgh had any weakness in the 1903 World Series, it was pitching. Right-hander Sam Leever had previously completed a great season for the Pirates with 25 game wins, including 7 shutouts, but by the season's end he was plagued by an ailing shoulder.

Another team standout was Charles Louis Phillippe. His clean lifestyle, in a time beset by drinking, swearing, and tobacco-chewing ballplayers, had earned him the nickname "Deacon" from his teammates. Joining the team in 1900, when Pittsburgh had merged with the Louisville

Colonels, he proved to be a phenomenal "control" pitcher who helped the Pirates win 25 games with only 9 losses in 1903. Phillippe would play a big role in the upcoming series.

In the previous two years, Ed Doheny had performed well on the mound for Pittsburgh. His 16 victories during the 1902 and 1903 seasons had won him a starting spot in the team's rotation. But during the last season he had begun showing signs of paranoia, at one point even leaving the team complaining that detectives were following him. Sadly, in October 1903, Doheny was committed to an asylum, creating a huge loss for the Pirates, as they prepared to for postseason play.

The starting catcher for Pittsburgh for postseason play was Eddie Phelps.

"Heart and soul" of the Pirates team was the shortstop Honus Wagner. Since coming to Pittsburgh in 1900, Wagner had amply proven his skill with a bat and glove and would grow to become one of baseball's great legends.

Honus Wagner

In his first year with the Pirates, Wagner won the National League batting title and led in triples and doubles. In 1903, he led the National League with a .355 batting average and, graced with lightning speed, nimbly found his way around infield bases. By the end of his playing career, in 1917, Wagner tallied 722 stolen bases. Although he played well in 1903, injuries had taken their toll by the second half of the season. Wagner would go into the World Series hampered by a swollen thumb and an injured right leg.

Making up the rest of the Pirates infield were outstanding players: Tommy Leach, third baseman; Claude Ritchey, second baseman; and William "Kitty" Bransfield, first baseman.

Nicknamed "Tommy the Wee" by fans, Leach stood only 5 feet 6 inches (167 centimeters) tall and weighed 135 pounds (61 kilograms).

In 1903, he batted .305 and led the National League with 6 home runs (the lowest number of home runs hit by a Major League team in a season during the 20th century).

Claude Ritchey proved to be a solid second baseman with exceptional speed around the bases.

In 1900, Fred Clarke joined the Pirates as right fielder and club manager. Clarke had all the makings of a great ballplayer — speed in the outfield and on the bases. As a left-handed line-drive hitter, he would achieve a lifetime batting average of .312 and tally 506 stolen bases in 16 years with the Pirates.

Clarence Beaumont, affectionately dubbed "Ginger" for his red hair, was the Pirates center fielder. He had performed so well for the Western

Tommy Leach

League that Pittsburgh purchased his contract in 1899. As a rookie for the Pirates, Beaumont batted .352.

Another left-handed hitter and starting right fielder for the Pirates was 21-year-old Jimmy Sebring. Sebring had joined the Pirates in 1903 and would prove to be a great asset in the approaching World Series.

On October 1, 1903, at Huntington Avenue Grounds in Boston, Massachusetts, the first World Series between a National League team and an American League team was about to commence and establish, from that day forward, the blueprint for all future World Series championships.

Crowd attendance was expected to be high, due to the much-anticipated return of postseason play.

On paper, both the Pirates and the Pilgrims appeared evenly matched, with the Pirates seen as the stronger of the two teams and the Pilgrims given the edge for pitching. Betting people everywhere were placing odds on the Pilgrims in the Series.

The Ballparks

Huntington Avenue Grounds — Home of the 1903 Boston Pilgrims

In 1901, "Ban" Johnson, founder of the new American League, formed a team in Boston to compete head-to-head with the Boston Nationals of the well-established National League.

Johnson quickly began building a ballpark for his new franchise. Its location was a former circus lot that bordered the New York, New Haven, and Hartford railroad maintenance yards on busy Huntington Avenue in Boston, Massachusetts. Located just a short distance from the lot, on the other side of the tracks, was the National League ballpark.

Within three months, Huntington Avenue Grounds ballpark was completed. Built to hold a crowd of 11,500 baseball fans, the park featured a spacious playing field with 90 feet (274 centimeters) of foul territory from the first and third base bags to the grandstands. From home plate to the backstop was a distance of 60 feet (183 centimeters).

Huntington Avenue Grounds ballpark opened on May 8, 1901, with Cy Young taking the pitcher's mound for the Boston Pilgrims against the Boston Nationals. Young and his team defeated the Nationals 12 to 4. In the ballpark's first year, more than 300,000 fans attended games at the Huntington Avenue Grounds, outdrawing the Boston Nationals ballpark 2 to 1.

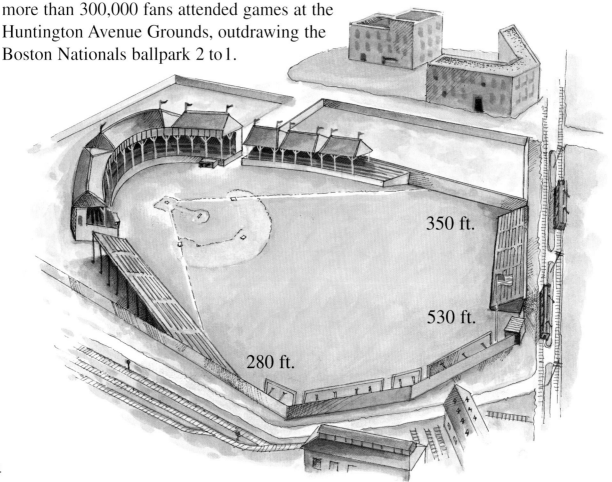

350 ft.

530 ft.

280 ft.

Exposition Park — Home of the 1903 Pittsburgh Pirates

Built by the Players League in 1890, Exposition Park was located on the north shore of the Allegheny River. The Pirates took ownership of the park in 1891, shortly after the collapse of the Players League.

Across the river from Exposition Park lay Pittsburgh, a city that, in 1903, led the country in production of iron, steel, and other raw materials needed by a growing nation. From the park, one could spy hundreds of smokestacks belching thick black soot at midday against the backdrop of the Pittsburgh skyline. Although the park was one of the most accessible in the Major Leagues, its location posed a problem. In July 1902, the Allegheny River rose over its banks and left a foot of water covering most of the outfield at Exposition Park.

One of the features that made Exposition Park unique was its twin spires, which rose up behind home plate and could be seen by people from across the river in Pittsburgh. The last game played at Exposition Park was on June 29, 1908. The Pittsburgh Pirates' Three River Stadium was located at the site of the old Exposition Park from July 16, 1970, to October 1, 2000.

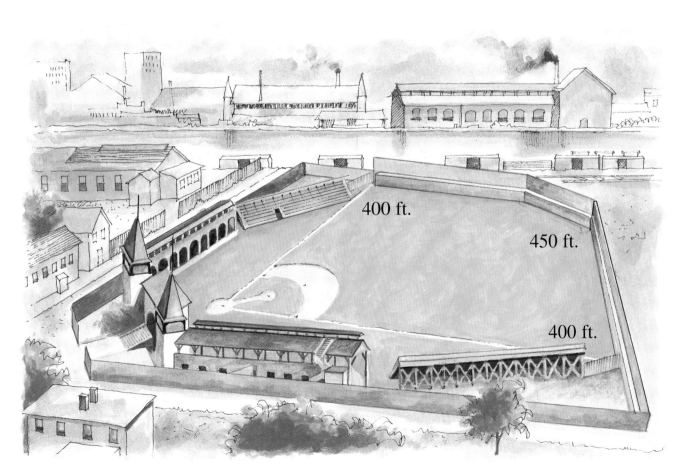

Chapter 6

1903
World Series Begins

Boston Pilgrims
vs
Pittsburgh Pirates

Huntington Avenue Grounds, Boston
October 1, 1903

Crowd attendance: 16,242 — With seating capacity at approximately 11,500, the overflow crowd is allowed to stand behind roped-off areas along outfield walls.

Score: Pirates, 7; Pilgrims, 3.

Behind home plate: Umpires: Hank O'Day (National League); Tommy Connolly (American League). They will officiate all 8 games.

On the mound: The great Cy Young is the starting pitcher for the Boston Pilgrims. He is racked for 4 runs in the first inning. He gives up 12 hits, 3 of them triples. Pitcher "Deacon" Phillippe for the Pirates strikes out ten batters and gives up only 6 hits.

At the plate: Pittsburgh's Jimmy Sebring, a left-handed hitter, hits the first home run in the Series. He has 3 hits in the game and drives in 4 runs. Third baseman Tommy Leach hits 2 triples in the game.*

Commentary: The Boston Pilgrims score twice in the seventh inning and once in the ninth inning on an error by shortstop Honus Wagner.

In the field: The Pirates defense is outstanding. Center fielder Clarence "Ginger" Baker and Fred Clarke track down a number of hard-hit balls in the outfield. Errors by Freeman, Ferris, and Criger of the Boston Pilgrims stun the overflow crowd at Huntington Grounds. Boston can't play any worse, and some fans even speculated that certain members of the team might have been paid by gamblers to lose the game.

---

*Both baseball teams and umpires agreed that any baseball hit into the outfield crowd standing alongside outfield walls would be deemed a "ground rule triple." This rule was upheld throughout the Series.

Game 4

Huntington Avenue Grounds, Boston
October 2, 1903

Crowd attendance: 9,415 — Attendance is down, due to the appearance of threatening inclement weather.

Score: Pilgrims, 3; Pirates, 0.

On the mound: The Pilgrims starting pitcher, Bill Dinneen, allows only 4 hits and strikes out 11, shutting down Pittsburgh batters. (Pittsburgh initially starts pitcher Sam Leever, but he's forced to leave early in the game, due to a sore arm. He's relieved by Frederick "Bucky" Veil.)

Turning point: Pat Dougherty, Pilgrims left fielder, hits a lead-off home run to center field in the first inning. Later in the game, Dougherty hits a second home run over the left field fence. (The next baseball player to hit 2 home runs in a World Series game is Harry Hooper of the Boston Red Sox in a game against the Philadelphia Phillies in 1915.)

In the field: In the fourth inning of the Series, Honus Wagner, shortstop for the Pirates, is robbed of a hit on a great catch by Pilgrims second baseman Albert "Hobe" Ferris, who then races to the second base bag to double up Fred Clarke.

Game 5

Huntington Avenue Grounds, Boston
October 3, 1903

Crowd attendance: 18,000 — 10,000 people are turned away at the gate. It is estimated that more than 1,000 people had climbed outfield walls and forced their way through ballpark entrances at the start of the game. Boston policemen, assisted by some of the baseball players, manage to contain the crowd along outfield walls by using rubber fire hoses as a barrier against determined fans. To avert a riot, fans are permitted to watch the game from positions along outfield walls.

Score: Pirates, 4; Pilgrims, 2.

On the mound: Pittsburgh pitcher "Deacon" Phillippe, winner of the first game for Pittsburgh, takes the mound having had only one day's rest. "Long Tom" Hughes, a 20-game winner in 1903, is starting pitcher for the Pilgrims. Hughes is knocked out in the third inning. Cy Young is brought in as a relief pitcher in the seventh inning, but Pittsburgh goes on to win game 3, by 4 to 2.

Turning point: When Cy Young appears in the seventh inning of game 3, 2 men are on base, with no outs. Young hits the first batter he faces, Honus Wagner. With the bases then loaded, the next hitter, Pirates first baseman "Kitty" Bransfield, pops up. Richey hits a grounder to third, and Clarke is forced out at home plate. Now, with 2 outs, Jimmy Sebring hits a ball to Jimmy Parent, shortstop for the Pilgrims. Parent boots the ball, and a third run crosses home plate for Pittsburgh. Wagner attempts to score but is thrown out at home plate.

Commentary: The Pilgrims are down 2 games to 1, and the World Series moves to Exposition Park in Pittsburgh, for the next 3 games. Most sportswriters are picking Pittsburgh to win the Series.

Game 4

Exposition Park, Pittsburgh
October 6, 1903 (This game was scheduled to be played on October 5 but was postponed due to rain.)

Crowd attendance: 7,600 — A light drizzle keeps the crowd size down.

Score: Pirates, 5; Pilgrims, 4.

On the mound: The Pirates return with pitcher "Deacon" Phillippe. This will be his third start in 6 days. Bill Dinneen is starting pitcher for Boston and already has one win in the Series.

At the plate: Three hits by Beaumont and Wagner and a 2-run triple by Tommy Leach give the Pirates a 5-1 lead going into the ninth inning. The only run for Boston comes on a single by Criger in the fifth inning.

A "BIG" rally: A large contingent of very vocal and fanatical Boston fans, who call themselves the "Royal Rooters," endure a roughly 20-hour train ride from Boston to cheer on their Pilgrims home team. Popular Boston saloon owner Mike McGreevey is their leader. Arriving along with the Rooters is a brass band. The wildly enthusiastic fans make such a racket during the ball game that afternoon newspaper writers credit the Royal Rooters for the Boston team's great comeback. Cheered on by the Rooters, the Pilgrims hit a cluster of singles at the top of the ninth inning to bring themselves within 1 run of the Pirates. With 2 outs and 2 men still on bases, pinch hitter Jack O'Brien pops up to the Pirates second baseman to end game 4. Elated Pirates fans pour onto the field to carry their hero, "Deacon" Phillippe, atop their shoulders.

Game 5

Exposition Park, Pittsburgh
October 7, 1903

Crowd attendance: 12,322 — The crowd is larger than that of the previous day, and the overflow is allowed to stand alongside outfield walls.

Score: Pilgrims, 11; Pirates, 2.

On the mound: Pittsburgh turns to Bill "Brickyard" Kennedy , who is celebrating his 36th birthday. There is much concern in Pittsburgh about Kennedy's ability to win this pivotal game. Kennedy has won only 13 games in his last 3 seasons in the Major Leagues. Although Cy Young lost game 1 for Boston, much of the loss is blamed on sloppy fielding by his teammates. Pittsburgh knows their team is facing the best pitcher in baseball.

Turning point: Kennedy and Young pitch scoreless baseball through the fifth inning, but in the sixth inning, the Pirates commit 3 errors (2 by Honus Wagner), allowing Boston to score 6 runs. During the sixth inning, left fielder Fred Clarke and shortstop Honus Wagner collide while chasing down a fly ball. Neither ballplayer can hear the other calling for the ball over the noise generated by the Royal Rooters and their brass band. Boston goes on to score 4 more runs in the seventh inning.

At the plate: Cy Young not only pitches a 5-hitter, but he helps his team by hitting a triple into the outfield crowd, driving in 2 runs. Patsy Dougherty hits a triple in the sixth inning. Boston trails in the Series by 3 games to 2.

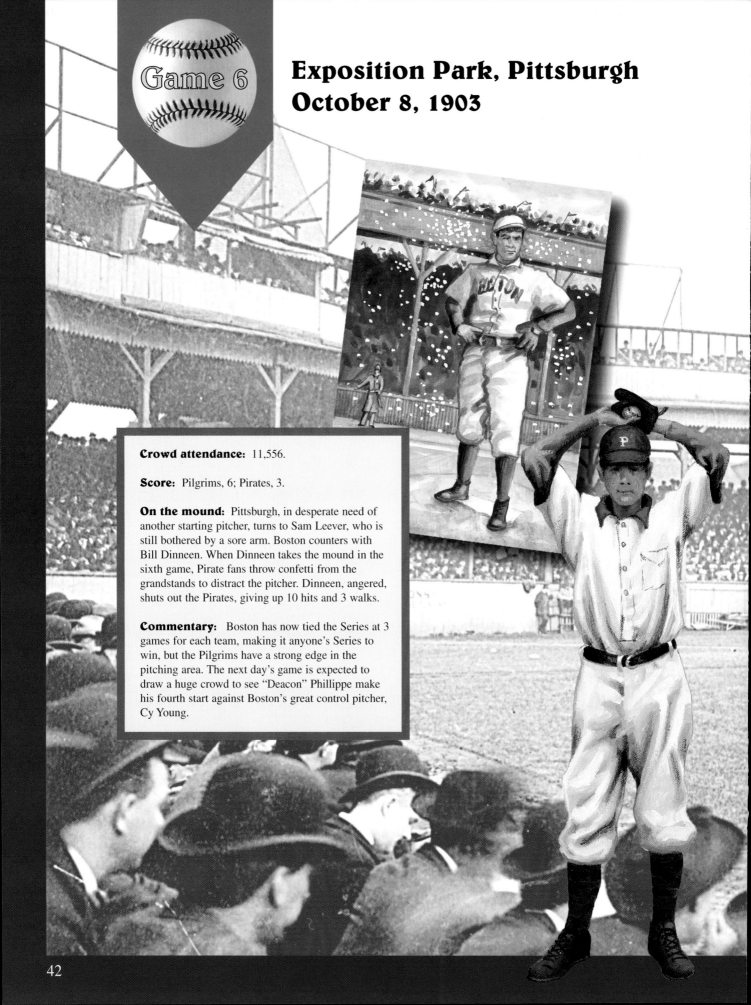

Game 6

Exposition Park, Pittsburgh
October 8, 1903

Crowd attendance: 11,556.

Score: Pilgrims, 6; Pirates, 3.

On the mound: Pittsburgh, in desperate need of another starting pitcher, turns to Sam Leever, who is still bothered by a sore arm. Boston counters with Bill Dinneen. When Dinneen takes the mound in the sixth game, Pirate fans throw confetti from the grandstands to distract the pitcher. Dinneen, angered, shuts out the Pirates, giving up 10 hits and 3 walks.

Commentary: Boston has now tied the Series at 3 games for each team, making it anyone's Series to win, but the Pilgrims have a strong edge in the pitching area. The next day's game is expected to draw a huge crowd to see "Deacon" Phillippe make his fourth start against Boston's great control pitcher, Cy Young.

Exposition Park, Pittsburgh
October 10, 1903 (This game was scheduled to be played on October 9 but was postponed due to bad weather.)

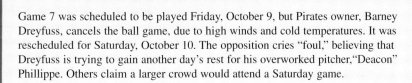

Game 7 was scheduled to be played Friday, October 9, but Pirates owner, Barney Dreyfuss, cancels the ball game, due to high winds and cold temperatures. It was rescheduled for Saturday, October 10. The opposition cries "foul," believing that Dreyfuss is trying to gain another day's rest for his overworked pitcher,"Deacon" Phillippe. Others claim a larger crowd would attend a Saturday game.

Crowd Attendance: Saturday, October 10, baseball fans arrive at Exposition Park early. By the start of the game, more than 17,038 fans fill the stands, forming a human wall along outfield walls. Thousands of fans have to be turned away for lack of room. Many fans observe the game from high elevations, like Monument Hill, around the ballpark. As the game begins, heavy black smoke from nearby steel mills blackens the sky above the ballpark, delaying the game.

Score: Pilgrims, 7; Pirates, 3.

On the mound: Cy Young makes his third start as pitcher for the Pilgrims, and "Deacon" Phillippe, his fourth, for the Pirates.

The game: By the fourth inning, Boston gives Cy Young a 4-run lead. It isn't until the bottom of the fourth inning that Pittsburgh scores its first run on a high chopper by Ritchey, who scores Bransfield. Boston scores 2 more in the sixth inning. At the bottom of the sixth inning, the Pirates score their second run. Wagner hits a ground ball to the mound, which Young fields cleanly and throws to first base for an out. The Pirates strand 9 base runners during the game. Phillippe clearly shows signs of being overworked and gives up 11 hits, 5 ruled as "ground rule triples."

Commentary: Boston makes a great comeback and leads the Series 4 games to 3. The Pilgrims can wrap up the Series in Boston with a win. A ninth game will be played in Boston if Pittsburgh ties up the Series.

Game 8

Huntington Avenue Grounds, Boston
October 13, 1903 (This game was scheduled to be played
on Monday, October 12 but was postponed due to bad weather.)

Crowd attendance: More than 7,000 loyal fans are on hand for the ball game, but the threat of more bad weather keeps many away. The Royal Rooters get the "royal" treatment because of their loyalty to the Pilgrims during the Series. They are seated in four rows of chairs positioned directly in front of the grandstand.

Score: Pilgrims, 3; Pirates, 0.

On the mound: A rested Bill Dinneen gets the pitching assignment for Boston. The Pirates once again counter with "Deacon" Phillippe, who's already pitched 4 complete ball games in the Series for 3 victories.

In the field: Pittsburgh is hurting. Second baseman Ritchey's throwing hand is swollen, due to an infection, and Wagner is nursing a painful arm injury.

Turning point: Bill Dinneen pitches a brilliant game. It's his second shutout of the Series. Dinneen retires the first 11 batters before giving up a walk. In the third inning, Dinneen, while grabbing a line drive with his pitching hand, splits open a finger and continues to pitch the entire game in this condition, leaving bloodstains on the ball. The Pirates' next chance to score comes in the fourth inning with Leach on third base and Wagner on first base. With 2 outs, Wagner takes off for second base on a delayed steal attempt. Pilgrims catcher Lou Criger bluffs a throw to second base and fires down to third base, catching Leach off the bag, ending the inning. Criger's defense shines again in the sixth inning, when he picks off Phillippe at first base.

The final inning: By the top of the ninth inning, Dinneen hasn't given up a hit since the sixth inning. There are no errors committed by the Pilgrims this day. Dinneen quickly retires Clarke and Tommy Leach for the first 2 outs. The great Honus Wagner steps up to the plate. Dinneen works him to a full count of 3 balls and 2 strikes. For the first time in the Series, the Royal Rooters are silent. There is no brass band playing and no singing of the popular song "Tessie"— just two great ballplayers facing off against each other to make baseball history. Dinneen delivers the final pitch. Wagner swings and misses a chest-high fast ball. Catcher Lou Criger throws the ball high into the air, as jubilant fans pour onto the ball field and lift their heroes aloft. Boston wins the first modern World Series in dramatic fashion.

Chapter 7

Conclusion

The first modern World Series was a huge success. More than 100,000 fans attended the 8-game fall epic. In many ways, it was a turning point for baseball. The professionalism and integrity that players demonstrated both on and off the ball field brought a new respectability to the game. Pirates owner Barney Dreyfuss said, "The Boston Club has won the World's Championship squarely, playing the cleanest kind of baseball."

As for the Royal Rooters led by saloon owner Mike McGreevey, there was no question that their loud cheering and constant singing of the song "Tessie" during the Series had played an important role in distracting Pirates players. Tommy Leach, Pirates third baseman, said of the Royal Rooters, "They sort of got on your nerves after a while. Before we knew what happened, we'd lost the World Series."

1903 World Series champions raise the victory flag at the Huntington Avenue Grounds at the beginning of the 1904 season.

Pitching had proved to be a deciding factor in the Series, as it would prove to be in many future World Series games. The outstanding pitching exhibited by both Bill Dinneen and Cy Young had contained the powerful Pirates lineup, and the heroic pitching effort of the Pirates pitcher "Deacon" Phillippe would not soon be forgotten. Throughout the Series, Phillippe pitched 44 innings, completing 5 games to win 3 in the contest. His total innings pitched, plus 5 complete games, are World Series records that stand to this day.

Even though the Pittsburgh players were under contract to play until October 15, Barney Dreyfuss generously shared all the money that he had made on the Series with his ballplayers, giving each a bonus of $1,300. This was not the case with the Boston players, whose contracts expired on September 30.

Pilgrims owner Henry Killilea had begrudgingly agreed to pay each player an extra week's salary to play in the Series, a total of $1,100 per player, but none of the ballplayers shared in the profits (more than $6,600) that Killilea had made from the Series. The losing team, the Pirates, had made more money for playing in the Series than the winning Boston Pilgrims.

The Pilgrims would go on to win another American League pennant in 1904, but there would be no World Series that year. That year, the pennant winner in the National League was the New York Giants, coached by the notorious John McGraw whose toughness and vulgarity on the playing field had made him a legend.

New York Giants owner John T. Brush, fearing that the rival New York Highlanders of the American League might overtake the Pilgrims at the end of the season, announced that the New York Giants would not participate in any postseason play. Although the Highlanders lost the pennant to the Pilgrims on the last day of the season, McGraw's Giants refused to play in a World Series.

Due to overwhelming demand by loyal baseball fans and sportswriters alike, the World Series resumed in 1905 and is still here today a century later.

Baseball had finally grown up in America. Never before had a game captured so much of the heart and soul of a nation. American poet Walt Whitman said it best: *"Well — it's our game; that's the chief fact in connection with it; America's game: It has snap, go, fling of the American atmosphere; it belongs as much to our institutions, fits into them as significantly as our Constitution's laws; is just as important in the sum total of our historic life."*

Bibliography

Allen, Lee. *The World Series.* New York: G. P. Putman's Sons, 1969.

Browing, Reed. *Cy Young: A Baseball Life.* Amherst: University of Massachusetts Press, 2000.

DeValeria, Dennis. *Honus Wagner: A Biography.* Pittsburgh: University of Pittsburgh Press, 1998.

Nemec, David. *Great Baseball Feats, Facts & Firsts.* New York: Signet Books, 1990.

Okkonen, Marc. *Baseball Memories 1900-1909: An Illustrated Chronicle of the Big League's First Decade.* New York: Sterling Publishing Co., Inc., 1992.

Redmount, Robert S. *The Red Sox Encyclopedia.* Champaign, IL: Sports Publishing, Inc. 1998.

Ritter, Lawrence S. *The Glory of Their Times: The Story of the Early Days of Baseball Told by the Men Who Played It.* New York: William Morrow, 1992.

Rossi, John P. *The National Game: Baseball and American Culture.* Chicago: Ivan R. Dee, 2000.

Seymour, Harold. *Baseball: The People's Game.* New York: Oxford University Press, 1990.

Stark, Benton. *The Year They Called off the First World Series: A True Story.* New York: Avery Publishing Group, Inc., 1991.

Stout, Glenn, and Richard A. Johnson. *One Hundred Years of Red Sox Baseball: Red Sox Century.* Boston: Houghton Mifflin Co., 2000.

Thorn, John. *Treasures of the Baseball Hall of Fame.* New York: Villard Books, 1998.

Ward, Geoffrey C., and Ken Burns. *Baseball: An Illustrated History.* New York: Alfred A. Knopf, 1994.

Wright, Russell. *A Tale of Two Leagues: How Baseball Changed as the Rules, Franchises, Stadiums and Players Changed, 1900−1998.* Jefferson, NC: McFarland & Company, Inc., 2000.

Contributing Writers: Hank Stephen Hanks, Perry Barber, Allen Barra, Thomas G. Gilbert, Joe Glichman, Owen Kean, Berry Stainback. *150 Years of Baseball.* New York: Beekman House, 1989.

Index

About the Author/Artist

Peter A. Campbell is a 1970 graduate of Vesper George School of Art, Boston, Massachusetts. His paintings have been exhibited throughout the East Coast and are represented in many private collections. He has won more than twenty painting awards and honors, including membership in the National Society of Painters in Casein and Acrylic in New York City. Peter is also a member of the Society of Children's Book Writers and Illustrators. Recently he was appointed to the Board of Directors of the Attleboro Museum in Attleboro, Massachusetts.

In 1989, Peter was selected by NASA to become a member of its space art program, which documents major aerospace activities by recording them in artwork.

That same year, he spent a week touring, sketching, and photographing the activities at the Kennedy Space Center in Florida. He also witnessed the exciting launch of the space shuttle Atlantis, *which carried the Venus probe* Magellan. *From the experience, Peter created the painting "Voyage to Venus," which now hangs in NASA's permanent art collection in Florida. Peter's space paintings have also been featured in* The Artist Magazine.

In 1995, The Millbrook Press published Peter's first children's book, LAUNCH DAY, which he wrote and illustrated. In 2000, Millbrook published his second book, ALIEN ENCOUNTERS.

Peter has also worked as an art director and creative director for several Rhode Island advertising agencies. He lives in Lincoln, Rhode Island, with his wife and their three sons Seth, Jeremy, and Brendan.

Author/artist photo by Brendan Campbell